The Harlem Renaissance

by Dana Meachen Rau

Content Adviser: Marcellus Blount, Ph.D.,
Associate Professor, Department of English and Comparative Literature,
Columbia University

Reading Adviser: Rosemary G. Palmer, Ph.D.,
Department of Literacy, College of Education,
Boise State University

COMPASS POINT BOOKS
MINNEAPOLIS, MINNESOTA

Compass Point Books
151 Good Counsel Drive, P.O. Box 669
Mankato, MN 56002-0669

Visit Compass Point Books on the Internet at *www.compasspointbooks.com*
or e-mail your request to *custserv@compasspointbooks.com*

On the cover: Harlem Renaissance artist Edward Burra painted this work, titled *Harlem, 1934*.

Photographs ©: Tate Gallery, London/Art Resource, NY, cover; Prints Old and Rare, back cover (far left); Library of Congress, back cover, 14, 20; Sid Grossman, Harlem Street Scene, 1939, Museum of the City of New York, Federal Arts Project, 5; Smithsonian American Art Museum, Washington, D.C./Art Resource, NY, 6, 35; Hulton Archive/Getty Images, 8, 30; Bettmann/Corbis, 9, 15, 23, 31, 33; Hansel Mieth/Time Life Pictures/Getty Images, 10; C.M. Battey/Getty Images, 12; MPI/Getty Images, 13; The Granger Collection, New York, 16; Robert W. Kelley/Time Life Pictures/Getty Images, 18; Yale Collection of American Literature, Beinecke Rare Book and Manuscript Library, 19; Conde Nast Archive/Corbis, 22; The New York Public Library/Art Resource, NY, 24; National Portrait Gallery, Smithsonian Institution/Art Resource, NY, 26; Schomburg Center, The New York Public Library/Art Resource, NY, 27; Frank Driggs Collection/Getty Images, 29, 32; Michal Daniel, 37; General Photographic Agency/Getty Images, 38; Genevieve Naylor/Corbis, 40; Scott Olson/Getty Images, 41.

Photo on page 19 reprinted by permission of Harold Ober Associates Incorporated

Editor: Jennifer VanVoorst
Designer/Page Production: Bradfordesign, Inc./The Design Lab
Photo Researcher: Marcie C. Spence
Cartographer: XNR Productions, Inc.
Educational Consultant: Diane Smolinski
Library Consultant: Kathleen Baxter

Managing Editor: Catherine Neitge
Creative Director: Keith Griffin
Editorial Director: Carol Jones

For Charlie and Allison, two creative souls

Library of Congress Cataloging-in-Publication Data
Rau, Dana Meachen, 1971–
  The Harlem Renaissance / by Dana Meachen Rau.
    p. cm. — (We the people)
  Includes bibliographical references and index.
  ISBN-13: 978-0-7565-1264-4 (hardcover)
  ISBN-10: 0-7565-1264-6 (hardcover)
  ISBN-13: 978-0-7565-1727-4 (paperback)
  ISBN-10: 0-7565-1727-3 (paperback)
  1. African-American arts—New York (State)—New York—20th century. 2. Harlem (New York, N.Y.)—Intellectual life—20th century. 3. Harlem Renaissance. I. Title. II. We the people (Series) (Compass Point Books)
  NX512.3.A35R38 2005
  700'.89'9607307471—dc22   2005002542

072009
005590R

TABLE OF CONTENTS

A Buzz in the Streets

It is night in the city. Listen. The whisper of a poet reading his work sneaks down from a window above. The blare of a trumpet and a tune from a singer fill the air. People gather outside talking about their hard day's work and, more importantly, what they are planning to do with their future.

This night is filled with voices—African-American voices during a time called the Harlem Renaissance. The Harlem Renaissance refers to the neighborhood of Harlem in New York City during the 1920s and 1930s, when literature, art, and music flourished in the black community. It was a time of creativity, when black people had something to say, and others were willing to listen.

Harlem was magical. "Harlem was not so much a place as a state of mind," wrote the poet Langston Hughes. The streets of Harlem were filled with a buzz of voices talking about new ideas and ways to express them. The

4

In the 1920s and 1930s, Harlem was a vibrant African-American community.

Harlem Renaissance was about creating art that could
be shared with others—both whites and blacks. Poems,
stories, music, theater, painting, and sculpture were ways
for African-Americans to share their ideas with the world.

African-Americans at this time were redefining
themselves. It had been rare up to this point in American
history that a black person was thought of as much beyond
a slave, servant, or hired hand. African-Americans wanted
to create a new identity as a people. Identity describes
where you come from and where you are going. It is

African-American artist William H. Johnson painted this Harlem street scene.

thinking about what you feel about yourself, and how you want others to see you.

The Harlem Renaissance was an exploration of ideas. People did this in different ways and did not always agree. But what was important was that all voices had the freedom to speak and all voices were heard.

HOME IN HARLEM

Until the early 1900s, most African-Americans lived in the Southern states. But between 1910 and 1920, African-Americans started leaving the South in large numbers. This movement is called the "Great Migration." They moved north to cities such as New York City, Chicago, and Washington, D.C.

Many left to look for a better life. For hundreds of years, African-Americans had worked on plantations in the South as slaves. Even when slaves were freed by the Emancipation Proclamation in 1863, African-Americans in the South continued to suffer. Many still farmed on white-owned land, but were not paid the same as white people who did the same jobs. They faced laws that segregated African-Americans from white people by keeping them out of the same restaurants and stores.

There were jobs in the Northern industrial cities because of World War I. Factories needed workers to make

African-Americans led a hard life in the rural South.

supplies. African-American farmers had just lived through seasons of droughts, floods, and insects that destroyed their crops. They were eager to leave the South.

Many African-Americans moved north to find work in city factories.

Harlem, a neighborhood in the upper part of New York City's Manhattan Island, attracted many of these new arrivals to the North. Philip Payton, an African-American who worked in real estate, urged white apartment owners there to rent their properties to African-Americans. The owners needed the money. They had built large apartment houses, but there was no one to live in them. Elsewhere in the city, the living conditions for African-Americans were horrible. Apartments were old, falling apart, and crowded.

African-Americans were drawn to the clean, new neighborhood of Harlem.

In Harlem, however, houses were new and streets were wide. African-American families began to move to Harlem.

The North still had its problems. Riots broke out, especially in crowded cities, where there were tensions between whites and blacks. There was segregation, and black people still worked as servants to white people. However, an African-American middle class began to form. Black people had access to better education and could get better jobs.

Harlem became known as the "Black Capital of the World." African-Americans from the South, the West

Indies, and elsewhere moved to this 2-square mile (5.2-square kilometer) neighborhood. Nowhere else in the world did so many African-Americans live in such a small area.

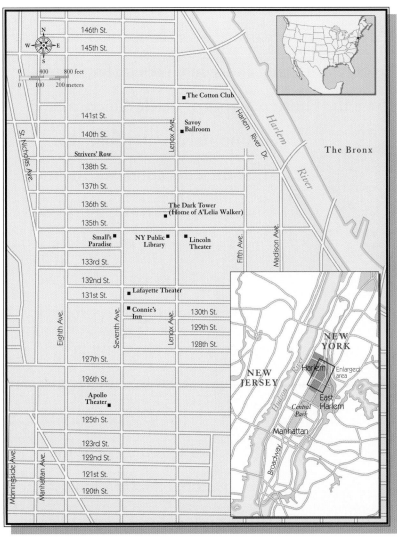

Harlem is located at the north end of the island of Manhattan.

A New Identity

At this time of change, African-Americans sought out leaders. W.E.B. DuBois was an outspoken supporter of rights for African-Americans. He was concerned about the relationship between black and white people. He wanted to break down the old stereotypes of black Americans as uneducated country folk. To him, education was the most important way for blacks to better themselves. He tried to show the intelligence, creativity, and diversity of African-Americans. DuBois was one of the founders of the National Association for the Advancement of Colored People

W.E.B. DuBois

12

NAACP representatives encouraged passersby to join their organization.

(NAACP) and was also the editor of their magazine, *The Crisis*. *The Crisis* gave African-American writers a chance to be published and share their ideas with readers.

Marcus Garvey

Another, very different leader during this time was Marcus Garvey. An energetic speaker from Jamaica, he created the Universal Negro Improvement Association (UNIA). He believed black people should return to Africa and create their own black nation there. While many people didn't agree with his ideas, Garvey worked hard in Harlem to unite African-Americans. He helped them find pride in their past and strength in their future through spirited parades and rallies.

A professor named Alain Locke also had a large influence on the Harlem Renaissance through a book

14

Members of the UNIA held parades to publicize their cause and gather support.

15

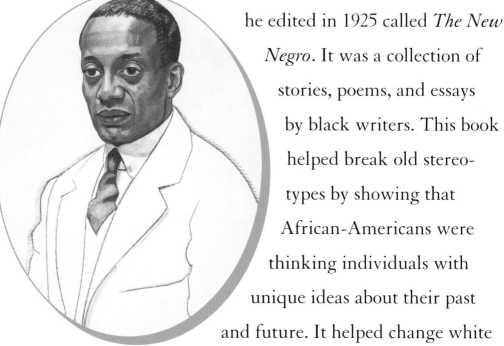

Alain Locke

he edited in 1925 called *The New Negro*. It was a collection of stories, poems, and essays by black writers. This book helped break old stereotypes by showing that African-Americans were thinking individuals with unique ideas about their past and future. It helped change white people's view of African-Americans by showing what they could contribute to the world.

The New Negro helped define the Harlem Renaissance. It was a call to the country that change was under way. The book became very popular among white readers in New York City. These citizens were becoming interested in the literature and other art that the previously unnoticed black community was beginning to produce.

WRITING DOWN THE PAST AND FUTURE

Literature by African-American authors flourished during the Harlem Renaissance. Many magazines, such as *The Crisis* and *Opportunity,* offered chances for black authors to be published. White publishers were more open to publishing books by black authors because their white audience, as well as the African-American middle class, was buying them. Black writers could finally express themselves and be heard. Readers all across the United States and even in Europe were interested in what black people had to say.

Langston Hughes was one of the most successful authors of the Harlem Renaissance. His work guided many writers of his time. His first book of poetry, *The Weary Blues,* was published in 1926. Hughes went on to write more poetry collections, short stories, plays, songs, and even children's books.

Langston Hughes

In his writings, Hughes explored the idea of what it meant to be black and American. He strongly believed that black artists—not only writers, but also painters, sculptors, actors, and musicians—should not create art merely to please white people. Hughes wrote, "We younger Negro artists who create now intend to express our individual dark-skinned selves without fear or shame. If white people are pleased, we are glad. If they are not, it doesn't matter. We know we are beautiful."

I've known rivers:
I've known rivers ancient as the world
and older than the flow of human blood
In human veins.

My soul has grown deep like the rivers.
I bathed in the Euphrates when dawns
were young.
I built my hut beside the Congo and
it lulled me to sleep.
I looked upon the Nile and raised the
pyramids above it.
I heard the singing of the Mississippi
when Abe Lincoln went down
to New Orleans,
and I've seen its muddy bosom
turn all golden in the sunset.
I've known rivers:
ancient, dusky rivers.
My soul has grown deep
like the rivers.

From memory to read
on radio show —
Langston Hughes

"The Negro Speaks of Rivers" was Langston Hughes' first nationally recognized poem.

Hughes was not afraid to write about the history of the black experience in the United States, as well as the new urban black life in Harlem. Many of his poems used the rhythm of jazz, a type of music popular in Harlem at the time. And the bustle of city life made his poems alive with a rhythm of their own.

Zora Neale Hurston, another writer of the Harlem Renaissance, was not so much influenced by the excitement of Harlem, but rather by looking to the past. Hurston went to school to be an anthropologist— someone who studies people and their culture.

Zora Neale Hurston

20

She scoured the South, talked to many people, and collected their traditional folktales. Hurston was often criticized by black thinkers of her time for not being more concerned with the future of black people in the United States. She was more interested in telling stories of the past. But by telling these stories, Hurston was preserving them. She was proud of her heritage, and she shared what blacks had to offer through their history.

ON STAGE AND IN PAINT

The theater had not been a friendly place for black people in the 19th century. African-Americans were portrayed in plays as simple and silly. Black characters were played by white actors who rubbed their faces with burnt cork to look "black."

During the Harlem Renaissance, however, African-American performers began to find their way on to the stage. They performed in vaudeville, a type of theater that presented long shows with many acts, including singers, comedians, and magicians. Other black actors performed in

22

Charles Gilpin

serious theater. Charles Gilpin was a popular and successful African-American actor. In 1916, he founded the Lafayette Players, a group of black actors in Harlem who performed at the Lafayette Theater.

The Lafayette Theater was Harlem's leading performance hall.

In 1921, an exciting event occurred for the black community. A musical comedy called *Shuffle Along* opened on Broadway, the theater district of New York

Shuffle Along *ran for 504 performances at Broadway's Cort Theatre.*

City. It was filled with memorable songs and dazzling dances. Most importantly, it was written and produced by African-Americans. All of the actors, singers, and dancers were black as well. The show was a success with both black and white audiences. *Shuffle Along* opened the stage for many more black actors and playwrights over the course of the decade.

At this time, African-American artists were also exploring new ideas and presenting them to the world. Painters and sculptors used their work to express their African history, Southern history, and the racial prejudices they experienced. They also found pride in the color of their skin. As W.E.B. DuBois wrote, "Let us train ourselves to see beauty in 'black.'" And that is what many artists did.

Aaron Douglas' paintings and illustrations are some of the most recognized of the Harlem Renaissance. He illustrated many magazine covers, book covers, and even murals on library walls. His flat

This contemporary portrait of Aaron Douglas hangs in the National Portrait Gallery.

colors and striking shapes drew on the style of African craftsmen. His subjects included current images of people dancing in night clubs, as well as historical ones, such as breaking the chains of slavery.

In 1925, Aaron Douglas wrote a letter to Langston Hughes. He shared his ideas about what black artists, whether they were painters, writers, or musicians, needed to do. Douglas wrote, "Let's bare our arms and plunge them deep through laughter, through pain, through sorrow, through hope, through disappointment, into the very depths of the souls of our people and drag forth material crude, rough, neglected. Then let's sing it, dance it, write it, paint it."

This detail from an Aaron Douglas painting depicts aspects of the African-American experience.

Jazzy Tunes and Dancing Feet

One could often hear the beat of music on a Saturday night in Harlem. The new type of music popular at the time was called jazz. People found it easy to dance to jazz. It had a steady drum beat and strong rhythm. Musicians even made up some of the tunes as they played. Piano players, called ticklers, became heroes in nightclubs. The thrilling sounds of big bands were in style. Musicians dressed in tuxedos and played trumpets, clarinets, drums, and more, while a bandleader kept time.

Duke Ellington was one of the most famous musicians of the Harlem Renaissance. He was a songwriter, piano player, and bandleader. He and his orchestra played at all the hottest spots in Harlem.

One of these hot spots was the Savoy Ballroom. It was called the "Home of Happy Feet" because it was the place to dance. The Savoy filled an entire block. Its huge

Duke Ellington and his band were famous throughout the world.

29

The Savoy Ballroom's neon signs lit up the Harlem night.

dance floor had bandstands on each end. When one
band stopped to take a break, another band started, so
music was always playing. Some people rested and ate

30

refreshments at tables around the edges while dancers filled the dance floor. The original swing dance, called the Lindy Hop, was created at the Savoy. Its bandstands not only attracted Duke Ellington, but many other jazz greats. Both white and black people danced the night away.

The Cotton Club was one of the most famous spots

Couples danced to big band music at the Savoy Ballroom.

in Harlem in the 1920s. It held huge floor shows with dancing and singing, while guests sat at tables to watch, drink, and eat fancy food. World-famous big bands played there. Its music was broadcast over the radio each week across the United States.

The Cotton Club was not for everyone, however. Only white people were allowed to watch the show.

32

The Cotton Club's front entrance was for white guests only.

At the Cotton Club, white guests danced to music performed by black musicians.

Black people were turned away at the door. The only black people allowed in the Cotton Club were waiters and performers.

Even though African-Americans enjoyed new freedoms during the 1920s, places like the Cotton Club were always cruel reminders of racism. Many white people came to Harlem to support the arts, but others came to Harlem because it was the thing to do. As they did with many fads, white people turned their interest away from black people soon after the decade ended.

PAYING THE RENT

The 1920s is sometimes called the "Roaring '20s." It was a carefree time, not only in Harlem, but in many cities. It was not always a happy time for African-Americans, however. Not everyone in Harlem expressed themselves as poets, writers, artists, or musicians. Most were working-class people. Many African-Americans worked in laundries or as hotel doormen or elevator operators. Some worked as peddlers, plodding through city streets with their pushcarts selling everything from fish and fruit to perfume and pickles. Many women worked as servants and housecleaners.

Rents were extremely high. The monthly rent for a Harlem apartment was up to $30 higher than elsewhere in New York City. Apartments were often crammed with people to help share the cost. Even with extra people to help pay the rent, many still found it difficult to come up with enough money.

34

This painting, titled The Janitor Who Paints, *shows the artistic feeling that ran through Harlem, even among African-Americans who were employed in other fields.*

To solve the problem, people held rent parties. They cleared out their furniture and borrowed chairs. The host charged admission. Guests paid between 25 to 50 cents at the door. Then inside, guests had to buy food and drinks. Rent parties were crowded, loud, and hot. More people meant more money for the host, so guests were not turned away. A piano player entertained as people danced and played cards. Parties often lasted until the next morning. Everyone had a good time, and the host earned enough money to help with that month's rent.

A'Lelia Walker was a great supporter of Harlem's art scene and one of the neighborhood's most famous party throwers. She invited Harlem's rich and famous to her grand affairs. Langston Hughes called her "the joy goddess of Harlem's 1920s." Walker was a tall woman who wore turbans and feathers on her head, dresses of silk and fur, and lots of jewelry. She was a millionaire with a home on 136th Street. Here she threw lavish parties and invited both black and white guests, including artists, publishers,

A scene from the musical Harlem Song *shows Harlem residents enjoying a rent party.*

and royalty from African and European countries. She
gathered together many great minds to share their ideas.
People could dance to the songs of the finest musicians
or retreat to the top-floor library to talk, read books, or
view artwork.

37

A'Lelia Walker (left) inherited her fortune from her mother's hair-care business.

Walker sent out hundreds of invitations, even though her home could only hold 100 people. Hughes wrote, "Her parties were as crowded as the New York subway at the rush hour—entrance, lobby, steps, hallway, and apartment a milling crush of guests with everybody seeming to enjoy the crowding."

ECHOES OF THE PAST

Black people had succeeded in redefining their image to America. While their history was filled with hardship, they approached their future with hope. They proved that art was a powerful way to communicate. They used their art to bridge the gap between whites and blacks and prove that everyone had something valuable to say.

This time of optimism did come to an end, however. One major reason was the Great Depression, which began in 1929. The whole country suffered. Many businesses and factories shut their doors, and millions of people lost their jobs. People in black communities, such as Harlem, were the first out of work. Money was scarce. In 1935, a riot broke out in Harlem. White shop owners and community members could not resolve their differences. Sadness replaced the good feelings and happy freedom of the earlier decade.

Harlem Renaissance artists, such as the one shown here, paved the way for black artists today.

Yet many say the Harlem Renaissance did not end. It opened many doors to African-American writers, artists, musicians, and entertainers. Publishers had become more open to work by black writers. Audiences still wished to see plays about the black experience. The sounds of jazz became the fabric of many future songs and styles of music. Aaron Douglas spoke of the role of African-Americans who would come after him: "We only lit the flame," he said. "We only set fire to this thing. But it's their business to take it, magnify it and to carry it on."

The Harlem Renaissance succeeded in changing the world's view of African-Americans. Many of its great figures lived on the streets of Harlem. Some just passed through. Others lived elsewhere. But they all helped Harlem put its mark on the world. Old stereotypes were finally broken. The Harlem Renaissance showed the world what the black community had to offer. The echoes of its many voices can still be heard today.

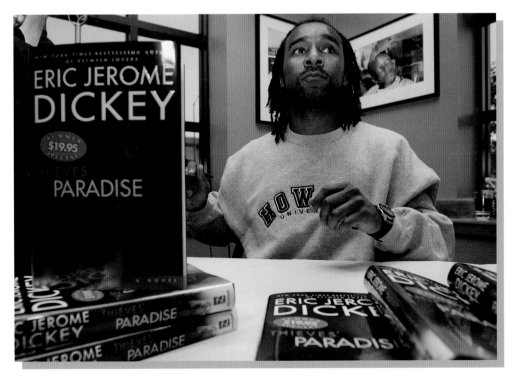

Author Eric Jerome Dickey is one of today's many new African-American voices.

GLOSSARY

craftsmen—people skilled at making things with their hands

Emancipation Proclamation—a document signed on January 1, 1863, by President Abraham Lincoln that freed slaves in the South

folktales—stories from the past that are often passed down orally

optimism—happiness and hopefulness

playwrights—people who write plays

racism—the belief that one group of people is better than another

rallies—large meetings organized to support a person or idea

segregated—separated from others because of race

stereotypes—simple views of other people without getting to know them individually

urban—having to do with a city

vaudeville—a type of theater that presented long shows with many acts, including singers, comedians, and magicians

DID YOU KNOW?

- When the subway line in New York City was extended to Harlem in the late 1800s, businessmen bought property there and built fancy apartments. They hoped people might want to move there to escape the busy city. But they had built too many too fast. The apartments in Harlem stood empty, waiting to be filled.

- The great jazz conductor Duke Ellington wrote more than 6,000 songs during his life, including the familiar "It Don't Mean a Thing (If It Ain't Got That Swing)."

- Langston Hughes' best-known poem, "The Negro Speaks of Rivers," was published in 1921—before he even went to college.

- During the 1920s, women cut their hair short and wore dresses to their knees, much shorter than ever before. They were called flappers because of the way their dresses flapped when they danced at parties.

- A'Lelia Walker called her home in Harlem "The Dark Tower" after Harlem Renaissance poet Countee Cullen's magazine column of the same name.

IMPORTANT DATES

Timeline

1903	Philip Payton makes a deal with white property owners to allow blacks to move into Harlem.
1909	NAACP founded.
1910– 1920	Southern blacks head north in the Great Migration.
1921	"The Negro Speaks of Rivers," Langston Hughes' best-known poem, is published.
1921	*Shuffle Along* opens on Broadway.
1923	The Cotton Club opens.
1924	Aaron Douglas moves to Harlem to paint.
1925	*The New Negro* by Alain Locke is published.
1927	The Savoy Ballroom opens.
1928	A'Lelia Walker begins to hold parties at her home in Harlem.
1929	The Great Depression begins.
1935	Riots break out in Harlem.

IMPORTANT PEOPLE

AARON DOUGLAS (1899–1979)

Painter whose art helped redefine the image of African-Americans

W.E.B. DUBOIS (1868–1963)

Educator and supporter of rights for African-Americans and one of the founders of the NAACP

DUKE ELLINGTON (1899–1974)

Bandleader, songwriter, and pianist who became famous in Harlem and around the world

CHARLES GILPIN (1878–1929)

Popular and successful actor who founded Harlem's Lafayette Players

LANGSTON HUGHES (1902–1967)

The most famous writer of the Harlem Renaissance, whose work includes poetry, stories, essays, songs, and plays

A'LELIA WALKER (1885–1931)

Millionaire known for her patronage of the arts as well as for the lavish parties she held in her Harlem home; she inherited her fortune from her mother, Madam C.J. Walker

WANT TO KNOW MORE?

At the Library

Haugen, Brenda. *Langston Hughes: The Voice of Harlem*. Minneapolis: Compass Point Books, 2006.

Hill, Laban Carrick. *Harlem Stomp! A Cultural History of the Harlem Renaissance*. New York: Megan Tingley Books, 2003.

Myers, Walter Dean. *Harlem*. New York: Scholastic Press, 1997.

Hughes, Langston. *The Dream Keeper and Other Poems*. New York: Alfred A. Knopf, 1996.

On the Web

For more information on this topic, use FactHound.

1. Go to *www.facthound.com*

2. Type in this book ID: 0756512646

3. Click on the *Fetch It* button.

FactHound will find the best Web sites for you.

On the Road

**The Anacostia Museum
and Center for African American
History and Culture**
1901 Fort Place S.E.
Washington, DC 20020
202/287-3306
To explore American history, society,
and creative expression from an
African-American perspective

**Schomburg Center for Research
in Black Culture**
The New York Public Library
515 Malcolm X Blvd.
New York, NY 10037-1801
212/491-2200
To visit changing exhibitions
about the experiences of
African-Americans

Look for more We the People books about this era:

Angel Island

The Great Chicago Fire

*Great Women of the
    Suffrage Movement*

The Haymarket Square Tragedy

The Hindenburg

Industrial America

The Johnstown Flood

The Lowell Mill Girls

Roosevelt's Rough Riders

A complete list of We the People titles is available on our Web site:
www.compasspointbooks.com

INDEX

About the Author

Dana Meachen Rau is an author, editor, and illustrator. A graduate of Trinity College in Hartford, Connecticut, she has written more than 100 books for children, including nonfiction, biographies, early readers, and historical fiction. She lives in Burlington, Connecticut, with her husband and two children.